CLASSIC ROCK FOR TWO

T0079050

Arrangements by Peter Deneff

ISBN 978-1-5400-6546-9

For all works contained herein:
Unauthorized copying, arranging, adapting, recording, Internet posting, public performance,
or other distribution of the music in this publication is an infringement of copyright.
Infringers are liable under the law.

Visit Hal Leonard Online at
www.halleonard.com

Contact Us:
Hal Leonard
7777 West Bluemound Road
Milwaukee, WI 53213
Email: info@halleonard.com

In Europe contact:
Hal Leonard Europe Limited
42 Wigmore Street
Marylebone, London, W1U 2RN
Email: info@halleonardeurope.com

In Australia contact:
Hal Leonard Australia Pty. Ltd.
4 Lentara Court
Cheltenham, Victoria, 3192 Australia
Email: info@halleonard.com.au

BANG A GONG

(Get It On)

CELLOS

Words and Music by
MARC BOLAN

Medium Rock

© Copyright 1971 (Renewed) Westminster Music Ltd., London, England
This arrangement © Copyright 2019 Westminster Music Ltd., London, England
R B Investments 1, Beverly Hills, CA controls all publication rights for the United States (administered by TRO-Essex Music International, Inc., New York, NY)
TRO-Essex Music International, Inc., New York controls all rights for Canada
International Copyright Secured
All Rights Reserved Including Public Performance For Profit
Used by Permission

CAN'T FIGHT THIS FEELING

CELLOS

Words and Music by
KEVIN CRONIN

Rock Ballad

Copyright © 1984 Fate Music (ASCAP)
This arrangement Copyright © 2019 Fate Music (ASCAP)
International Copyright Secured   All Rights Reserved

CARRY ON WAYWARD SON

CELLOS

Words and Music by
KERRY LIVGREN

Moderate Rock

Copyright © 1976 EMI Blackwood Music Inc.
Copyright Renewed
This arrangement Copyright © 2019 EMI Blackwood Music Inc.
All Rights Adminstered by Sony/ATV Music Publishing LLC, 424 Church Street, Suite 1200, Nashville, TN 37219
International Copyright Secured   All Rights Reserved

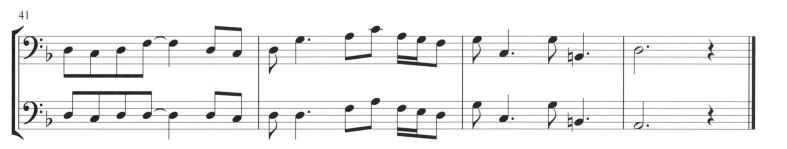

COLD AS ICE

CELLOS

Words and Music by MICK JONES
and LOU GRAMM

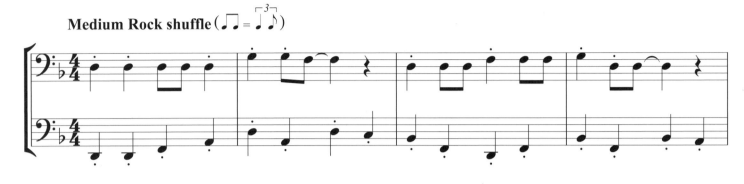

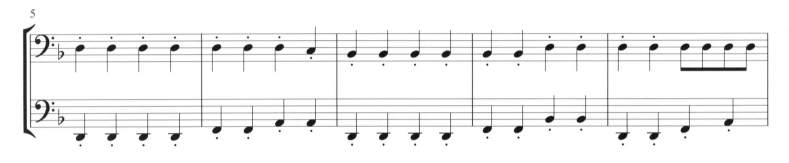

Copyright © 1977 Somerset Songs Publishing, Inc.
Copyright Renewed
This arrangement Copyright © 2019 Somerset Songs Publishing, Inc.
International Copyright Secured   All Rights Reserved

22

26
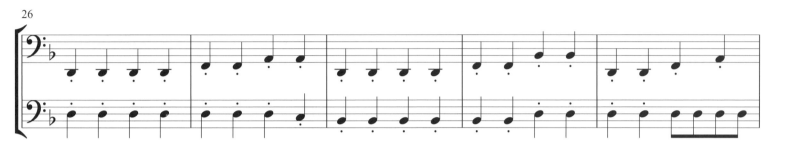

31

35

39

43

COME ON EILEEN

CELLOS

Words and Music by KEVIN ROWLAND,
JAMES PATTERSON and KEVIN ADAMS

Moderately

Copyright © 1982 EMI Music Publishing Ltd.
This arrangement Copyright © 2019 EMI Music Publishing Ltd.
All Rights Administered by Sony/ATV Music Publishing LLC, 424 Church Street, Suite 1200, Nashville, TN 37219
International Copyright Secured   All Rights Reserved

COME TOGETHER

CELLOS

Words and Music by JOHN LENNON
and PAUL McCARTNEY

Moderately

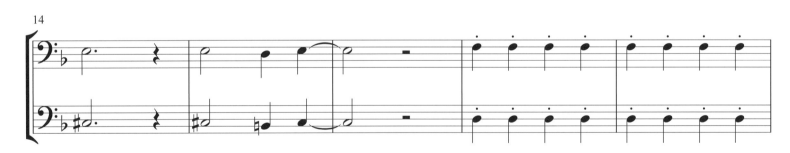

Copyright © 1969 Sony/ATV Music Publishing LLC
Copyright Renewed
This arrangment Copyright © Sony/ATV Music Publishing LLC
All Rights Administered by Sony/ATV Music Publishing LLC, 424 Church Street, Suite 1200, Nashville, TN 37219
International Copyright Secured   All Rights Reserved

CROCODILE ROCK

CELLOS

Words and Music by ELTON JOHN
and BERNIE TAUPIN

Lively

Copyright ©1972 UNIVERSAL/DICK JAMES MUSIC LTD.
Copyright Renewed
This arrangement Copyright © 2019 UNIVERSAL/DICK JAMES MUSIC LTD.
All Rights in the United States and Canada Controlled and Administered by UNIVERSAL - SONGS OF POLYGRAM INTERNATIONAL, INC.
All Rights Reserved   Used by Permission

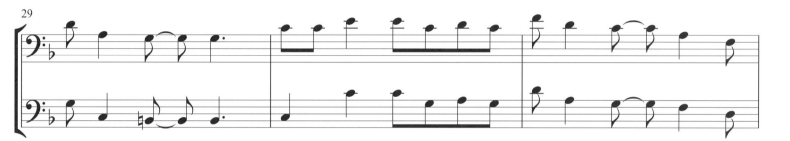

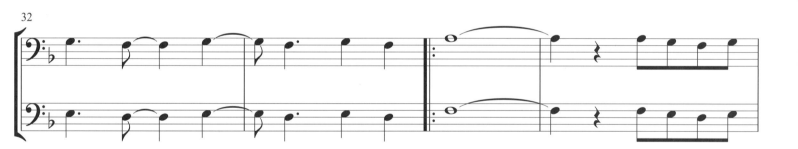

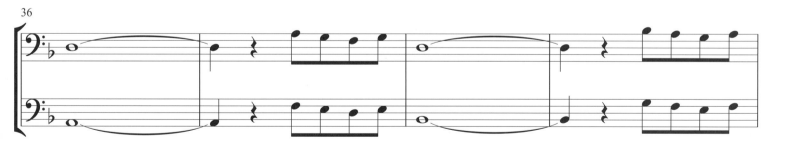

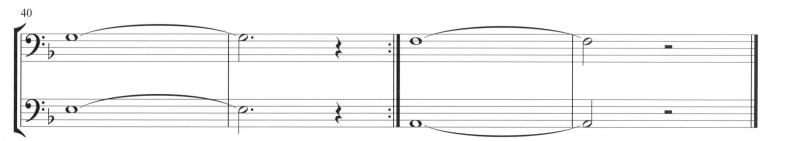

DOWN ON THE CORNER

CELLOS

Words and Music by
JOHN FOGERTY

Moderately

Copyright © 1969 Jondora Music c/o Concord Music Publishing
Copyright Renewed
This arrangement Copyright © 2019 Jondora Music c/o Concord Music Publishing
International Copyright Secured   All Rights Reserved

EVERY LITTLE THING SHE DOES IS MAGIC

CELLOS

Words and Music by
STING

Moderately fast

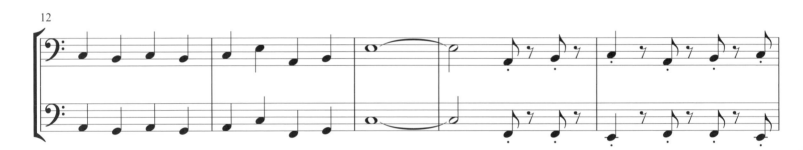

Copyright © 1981 G.M. Sumner
This arrangement Copyright © 2019 G.M. Sumner
All Rights Administered by Sony/ATV Music Publishing LLC, 424 Church Street, Suite 1200, Nashville, TN 37219
International Copyright Secured   All Rights Reserved

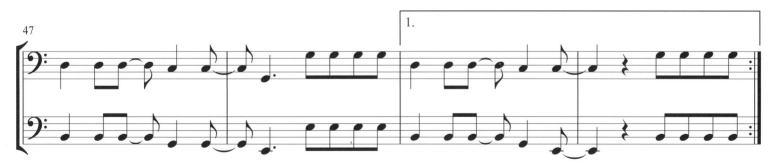

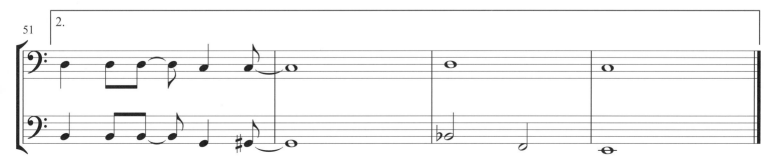

FREE FALLIN'

CELLOS

Words and Music by TOM PETTY
and JEFF LYNNE

Medium Rock

Copyright © 1989 Gone Gator Music and EMI April Music Inc.
This arrangment Copyright © 2019 Gone Gator Music and EMI April Music Inc.
All Rights for EMI April Music Inc. Administered by Sony/ATV Music Publishing LLC, 424 Church Street, Suite 1200, Nashville, TN 37219
All Rights Reserved   Used by Permission

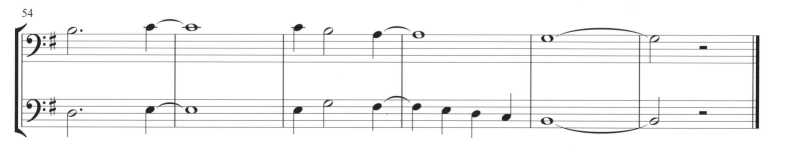

HURTS SO GOOD

CELLOS

Words and Music by JOHN MELLENCAMP
and GEORGE GREEN

Moderate Rock

Copyright © 1982 EMI Full Keel Music
This arrangement Copyright © 2019 EMI Full Keel Music
All Rights Administered by Sony/ATV Music Publishing LLC, 424 Church Street, Suite 1200, Nashville, TN 37219
International Copyright Secured   All Rights Reserved

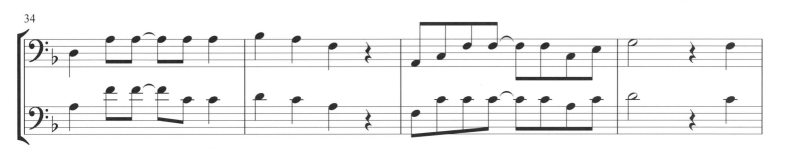

THE JOKER

CELLOS

Words and Music by STEVE MILLER,
EDDIE CURTIS and AHMET ERTEGUN

Copyright © 1973 by Sailor Music, Jim Rooster Music and Warner-Tamerlane Publishing Corp.
Copyright Renewed
This arrangement Copyright © 2019 by Sailor Music, Jim Rooster Music and Warner-Tamerlane Publishing Corp.
All Rights for Jim Rooster Music Administered Worldwide by Sailor Music
All Rights Reserved   Used by Permission

LIVIN' ON A PRAYER

CELLOS

Words and Music byJON BON JOVI,
DESMOND CHILD and RICHIE SAMBORA

Moderate Rock

Copyright © 1986 UNIVERSAL MUSIC PUBLISHING INTERNATIONAL LTD., BON JOVI PUBLISHING,
UNIVERSAL - POLYGRAM INTERNATIONAL PUBLISHING, INC., SONY/ATV MUSIC PUBLISHING LLC and AGGRESSIVE MUSIC
This arrangement Copyright © 2019 UNIVERSAL MUSIC PUBLISHING INTERNATIONAL LTD., BON JOVI PUBLISHING,
UNIVERSAL - POLYGRAM INTERNATIONAL PUBLISHING, INC., SONY/ATV MUSIC PUBLISHING LLC and AGGRESSIVE MUSIC
All Rights for UNIVERSAL MUSIC PUBLISHING INTERNATIONAL LTD. and BON JOVI PUBLISHING Administered by UNIVERSAL MUSIC WORKS
All Rights for SONY/ATV MUSIC PUBLISHING LLC and AGGRESSIVE MUSIC Administered by
SONY/ATV MUSIC PUBLISHING LLC, 424 Church Street, Suite 1200, Nashville, TN 37219
All Rights Reserved   Used by Permission

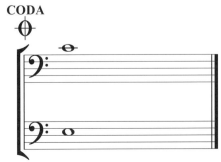

MAGGIE MAY

CELLOS

Words and Music by ROD STEWART
and MARTIN QUITTENTON

Copyright © 1971 by EMI Full Keel Music, Rod Stewart and Unichappell Music Inc.
Copyright Renewed
This arrangement Copyright © 2019 by EMI Full Keel Music, Rod Stewart and Unichappell Music Inc.
All Rights on behalf of EMI Full Keel Music and Rod Stewart Administered by Sony/ATV Music Publishing LLC,
424 Church Street, Suite 1200, Nashville, TN 37219
International Copyright Secured   All Rights Reserved

MR. ROBOTO

CELLOS

Words and Music by
DENNIS DeYOUNG

Copyright © 1983 by Stygian Songs
This arrangement Copyright © 2019 by Stygian Songs
International Copyright Secured   All Rights Reserved

Play 3 times

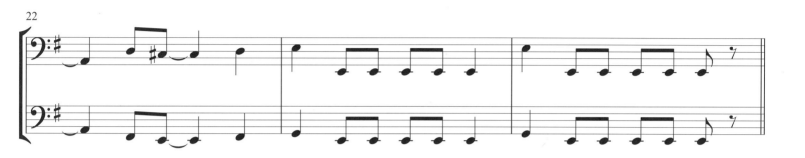

MONEY FOR NOTHING

CELLOS

Words and Music by MARK KNOPFLER
and STING

Moderate Rock

Copyright © 1985 STRAITJACKET SONGS LIMITED and G.M. SUMNER
This arrangment Copyright © 2019 STRAITJACKET SONGS LIMITED and G.M. SUMNER
All Rights for STRAITJACKET SONGS LIMITED Controlled and Administered by ALMO MUSIC CORP.
All Rights for G.M. SUMNER Administered by Sony/ATV Music Publishing LLC, 424 Church Street, Suite 1200, Nashville, TN 37219
All Rights Reserved   Used by Permission

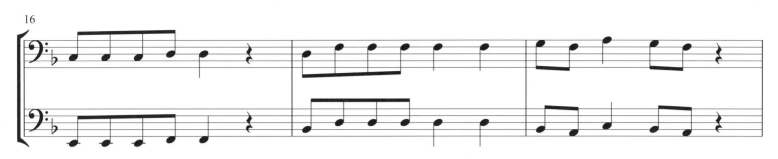

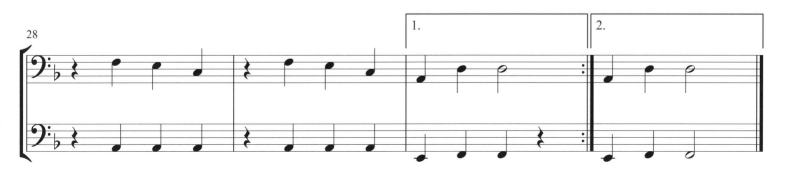

ONE MORE NIGHT

CELLOS

Words and Music by
PHIL COLLINS

Moderate Ballad

Copyright © 1985 Phil Collins Ltd.
This arrangement Copyright © Phil Collins Ltd.
All Rights Administered by Concord Sounds c/o Concord Music Publishing
All Rights Reserved   Used by Permission

PEACE OF MIND

CELLOS

Words and Music by
TOM SCHOLZ

Copyright © 1976 Pure Songs
Copyright Renewed
This arrangement Copyright © 2019 Pure Songs
All Rights Administered by Next Decade Entertainment, Inc.
All Rights Reserved   Used by Permission

REELING IN THE YEARS

CELLOS

Words and Music by WALTER BECKER
and DONALD FAGEN

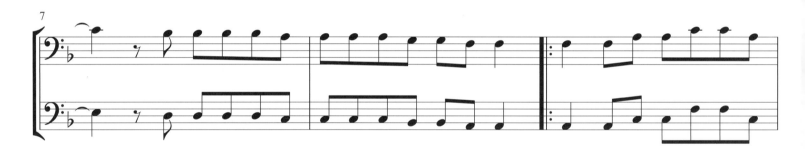

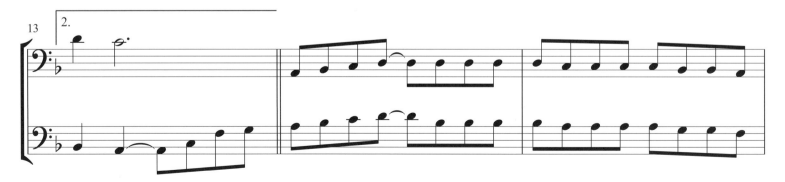

Copyright © 1972, 1973 UNIVERSAL MUSIC CORP. and RED GIANT, INC.
Copyrights Renewed
This arrangement Copyright © 2019 UNIVERSAL MUSIC CORP. and RED GIANT, INC.
All Rights Controlled and Administered by UNIVERSAL MUSIC CORP.
All Rights Reserved   Used by Permission

SMOKE ON THE WATER

CELLOS

Words and Music by RITCHIE BLACKMORE,
IAN GILLAN, ROGER GLOVER,
JON LORD and IAN PAICE

Moderate Rock

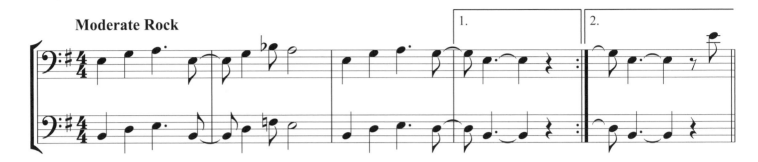

Copyright © 1972 B. Feldman & Co. Ltd.
Copyright Renewed
This arrangement Copyright © 2019 B. Feldman & Co. Ltd.
All Rights Administered by Sony/ATV Music Publishing LLC, 424 Church Street, Suite 1200, Nashville, TN 37219
International Copyright Secured   All Rights Reserved

SUMMER OF '69

CELLOS

Words and Music by BRYAN ADAMS
and JIM VALLANCE

Moderate Rock

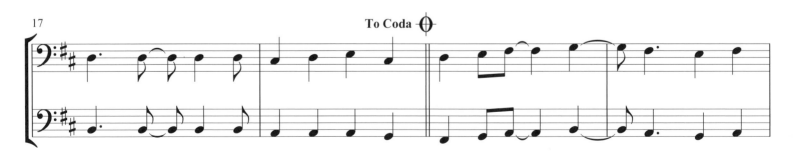

Copyright © 1984 IRVING MUSIC, INC., ADAMS COMMUNICATIONS, INC., ALMO MUSIC CORP. and TESTATYME MUSIC
This arrangement Copyright © 2019 IRVING MUSIC, INC., ADAMS COMMUNICATIONS, INC. ALMO MUSIC CORP. and TESTATYME MUSIC
All Rights for ADAMS COMMUNICATIONS, INC. Controlled and Administered by IRVING MUSIC INC.
All Rights for TESTATYME MUSIC Controlled and Administered by ALMO MUSIC CORP.
All Rights Reserved   Used by Permission

21

25

29

33
D.C. al Coda

CODA

36

40

UPTOWN GIRL

CELLOS

Words and Music by
BILLY JOEL

Moderately

Copyright © 1983 JOELSONGS
This arrangement Copyright © 2019 JOELSONGS
All Rights Administered by ALMO MUSIC CORP.
All Rights Reserved   Used by Permission

YOU'RE THE INSPIRATION

CELLOS

Words and Music by PETER CETERA
and DAVID FOSTER

Copyright © 1984 by Universal Music - MGB Songs and Peermusic III, Ltd.
This arrangement Copyright © 2019 by Universal Music - MGB Songs and Peermusic III, Ltd.
International Copyright Secured   All Rights Reserved

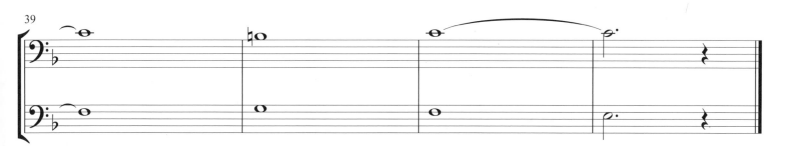

HAL LEONARD PRESENTS

EASY INSTRUMENTAL DUETS

Start your duet playing experience with these fun songbooks! Over 20 easy duet arrangements for two instrumentalists are featured in each of these collections. Woodwind and brass editions can be played together as can the string editions. **Only $9.99 each!**

THE BEATLES FOR TWO

23 favorites from the Fab Four in easy duet arrangements for two instrumentalists are featured in this collection: All You Need Is Love • Eleanor Rigby • Here Comes the Sun • Hey Jude • I Want to Hold Your Hand • Penny Lane • Something • Yellow Submarine • Yesterday • and more.

00291024	FLUTE	00291028	TROMBONE
00291025	CLARINET	00291029	VIOLIN
00291026	ALTO SAX	00291030	CELLO
00291027	TRUMPET		

BROADWAY SONGS FOR TWO

22 showstoppers: Any Dream Will Do • Bring Him Home • Cabaret • Edelweiss • For Forever • Hello, Dolly! • I Believe • Memory • One • Popular • Seasons of Love • Seventy Six Trombones • Tomorrow • Where Is Love? • You've Got a Friend • and more.

00252493	FLUTE	00252497	TROMBONE
00252494	CLARINET	00252500	VIOLIN
00252495	ALTO SAX	00252501	CELLO
00252496	TRUMPET		

CHRISTMAS CAROLS FOR TWO

Songs include: Angels We Have Heard on High • Away in a Manger • Deck the Hall • Jingle Bells • Joy to the World • O Holy Night • Silent Night • We Wish You a Merry Christmas • and more.

00277964	FLUTE	00277968	TROMBONE
00277965	CLARINET	00277969	VIOLIN
00277966	ALTO SAX	00277970	CELLO
00277967	TRUMPET		

HAL•LEONARD®

CHRISTMAS HITS FOR TWO

22 terrific holiday duets: All I Want for Christmas Is You • Baby, It's Cold Outside • The Christmas Song (Chestnuts Roasting on an Open Fire) • Do You Want to Build a Snowman? • Feliz Navidad • Have Yourself a Merry Little Christmas • It's Beginning to Look like Christmas • Let It Snow! Let It Snow! Let It Snow! • Mary, Did You Know? • Rockin' Around the Christmas Tree • Silver Bells • White Christmas • and more.

00172461	FLUTE	00172465	TROMBONE
00172462	CLARINET	00172466	VIOLIN
00172463	ALTO SAX	00172467	CELLO
00172464	TRUMPET		

CLASSIC ROCK FOR TWO

23 classic rock songs: Bang a Gong (Get It On) • Can't Fight This Feeling • Carry on Wayward Son • Cold As Ice • Come on Eileen • Come Together • Crocodile Rock • Down on the Corner • Every Little Thing She Does Is Magic • Free Fallin' • Hurts So Good • The Joker • Livin' on a Prayer • and more.

00303026	FLUTE	00303030	TROMBONE
00303027	CLARINET	00303031	VIOLIN
00303028	ALTO SAX	00303032	CELLO
00303029	TRUMPET		

CLASSICAL THEMES FOR TWO

24 favorite melodies from top classical composers: Air on the G String • Blue Danube Waltz • Canon in D • Eine Kleine Nachtmusik • Hallelujah Chorus • Jesu, Joy of Man's Desiring • Minuet in G Major • Ode to Joy • Pictures at an Exhibition • Sheep May Safely Graze • Trumpet Voluntary • William Tell Overture • and more.

00254439	FLUTE	00254443	TROMBONE
00254440	CLARINET	00254444	VIOLIN
00254441	ALTO SAX	00254445	CELLO
00254442	TRUMPET		

Prices, contents and availability subject to change without notice. Sales restrictions to some countries apply. All prices listed in U.S. funds.

DISNEY SONGS FOR TWO

23 Disney favorites: Beauty and the Beast • Circle of Life • Evermore • Friend Like Me • How Far I'll Go • Let It Go • Mickey Mouse March • Supercalifragilisticexpialidocious • When You Wish upon a Star • A Whole New World • Zip-A-Dee-Doo-Dah • and more.

00284643	FLUTE	00284647	TROMBONE
00284644	CLARINET	00284648	VIOLIN
00284645	ALTO SAX	00284649	CELLO
00284646	TRUMPET		

HIT SONGS FOR TWO

22 mega hits: All About That Bass • All of Me • Brave • Can't Stop the Feeling • Grenade • Hey, Soul Sister • I Will Wait • Let Her Go • 100 Years • Royals • Shake It Off • Shape of You • Stay with Me • Viva La Vida • and more.

00252482	FLUTE	00252486	TROMBONE
00252483	CLARINET	00252487	VIOLIN
00252484	ALTO SAX	00252488	CELLO
00252485	TRUMPET		

MOVIE SONGS FOR TWO

23 blockbuster hits are featured in this collection: City of Stars • Footloose • Hallelujah • Moon River • The Pink Panther • Puttin' on the Ritz • Skyfall • That's Amore • and more.

00284651	FLUTE	00284655	TROMBONE
00284652	CLARINET	00284656	VIOLIN
00284653	ALTO SAX	00284657	CELLO
00284654	TRUMPET		

POP CLASSICS FOR TWO

23 classic pop hits: Africa • Alone • Can't Smile Without You • Centerfold • Dancing Queen • Dust in the Wind • Every Breath You Take • Eye of the Tiger • I Melt with You • I Still Haven't Found What I'm Looking For • Imagine • Jessie's Girl • and more.

00303019	FLUTE	00303023	TROMBONE
00303020	CLARINET	00303024	VIOLIN
00303021	ALTO SAX	00303025	CELLO
00303022	TRUMPET		

ORDER TODAY FROM YOUR FAVORITE MUSIC RETAILER AT HALLEONARD.COM